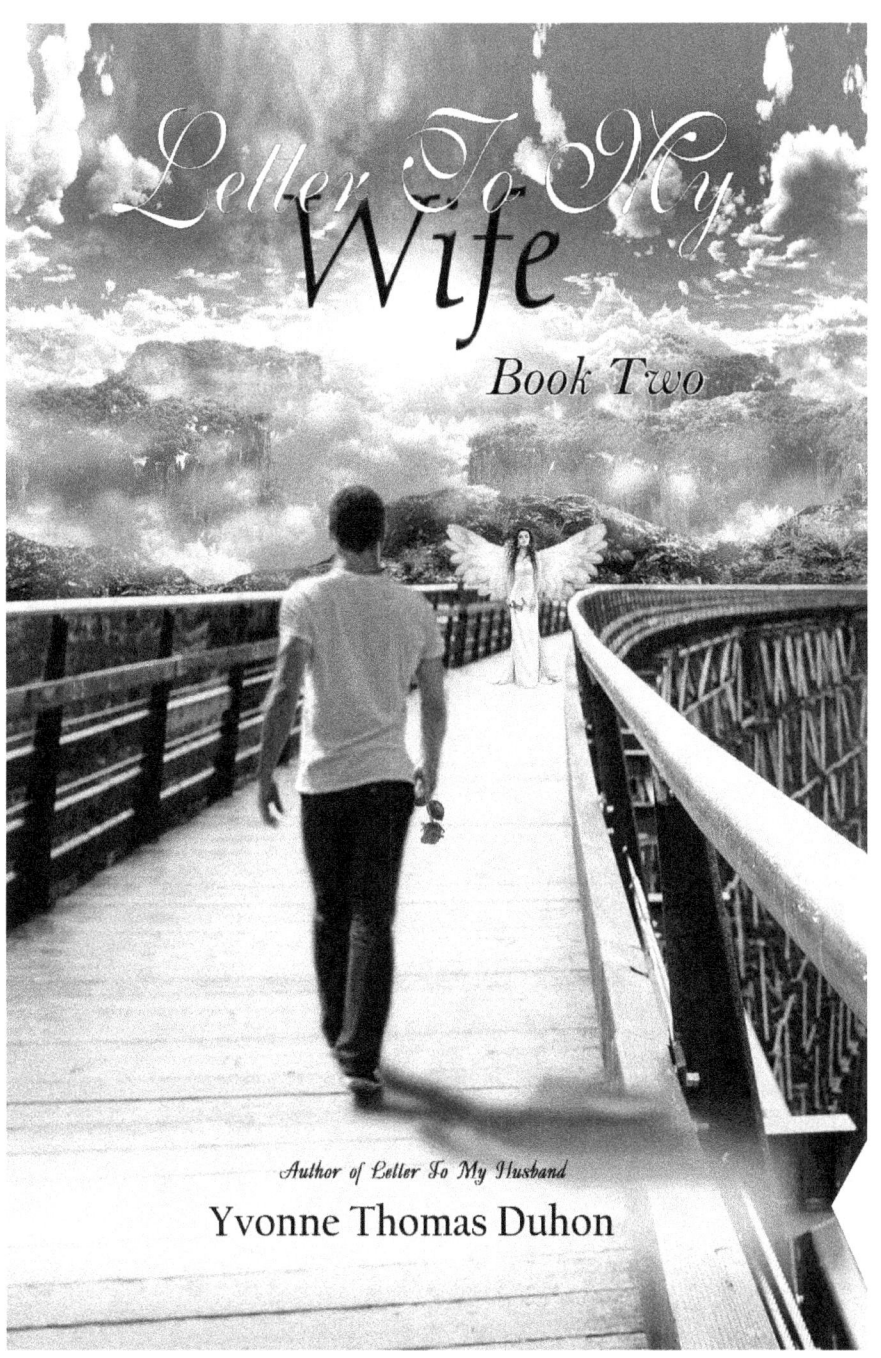

Letter to My Wife

Book Two

Yvonne Thomas Duhon

Pearly Gates Publishing, LLC, Houston, Texas

Letter to My Wife

Copyright © 2018
Yvonne Thomas Duhon

All Rights Reserved.
No portion of this publication may be reproduced, stored in any electronic system, or transmitted in any form or by any means (electronic, mechanical, photocopy, recording, or otherwise) without written permission from the publisher. Brief quotations may be used in literary reviews.

ISBN 13: 978-1-945117-84-8
Library of Congress Control Number: 2017964562

Scriptures marked NIV are used with permission from Zondervan via Biblegateway.com.

For information and bulk ordering, contact:
Pearly Gates Publishing, LLC
Angela Edwards, CEO
P.O. Box 62287
Houston, TX 77205
BestSeller@PearlyGatesPublishing.com

Acknowledgments

First and foremost, I give all praise, honor, and glory to God for using me as a vessel, working through me to share such a powerful and inspirational message to the world. I pray it blesses all who read it.

I give special honor to my Pastor, Dr. Ricky E. Carter, who has been a vital part of my spiritual development and who has always rightly-divided the Word of truth. Because of your teachings, I am now able to inspire, encourage, and reach others through my words — just as you have done for me.

Also, a very special "Thank You" to Minister Dwayne Simon and his beautiful wife, Valerie, for assisting me with setting the tone in the beginning of this book.

Thank you to the many family members and friends who provided support and encouragement to me throughout the journey of writing this book. I thank you so very much I couldn't have done it without you.

Last, but not least, to my five beautiful children: Kelli, Kaleb, Keith, Logan, and Laila: You have seen me at my best and at my worst. You are all a part of this journey with me. It's partly because of you that I am who I am and where I am today. I'm so proud to be your mom and that you are able to see God turn my test into a testimony. Never give up on God. He hears your prayers and His timing is always perfect!

Table of Contents

Acknowledgments vi

Letter to My Wife 1

    Proverbs 18:22 (NIV) 4

    Psalm 127:3 (NIV) 9

    Psalm 139:13-14 (NIV) 13

    Exodus 14:14 (NIV) 18

    1 Peter 5:7 (NIV) 23

    1 John 1:9 (NIV) 29

    Luke 11:28 (NIV) 32

    Matthew 5:4 (NIV) 36

About the Author 38

Yvonne Thomas Duhon

Letter to My Wife

Dear Wife,

Just like you, little did I know the path my life was about to take as well. When I first laid eyes upon you, I saw an angel sent from Heaven above. I know that may sound cheesy, but that's what I felt. I lit up like a teenager who had just had his first crush. Chills ran down my back. I couldn't get you out of my mind. I found myself wanting to see you again and again, not fully understanding why. I had to keep coming back to that diner you managed for my weekly lunches just to get a glimpse of you, hoping that it wasn't too busy so that I could request for you to come to my table to tell you how good the food tasted. Truth be told, I just wanted to say "Hi" and try to muster up the courage to ask you out.

There were moments when I was at a loss for words because looking at you made me literally lose every thought in my mind. Before I knew it, my weekly lunches turned into almost daily lunches. Sometimes, I would even come in for a cup of coffee on the weekend. I wasn't much of a breakfast person, but a cup of coffee and seeing you those mornings gave me a pep in my step for that day. I wasn't able to converse with you every time, but when I did, it gave me the opportunity to say a few more words with each visit, eventually working up the nerve to ask you out.

Even though you shut me down those first few times, I refused to give up. I knew that anything worth having was definitely worth waiting for! Each time I would ask you out, my pulse would race, I would stutter over my words, the palms of my hands would get sweaty, and I would have knots in my stomach—all while trying to look calm and cool on the outside. Finally, you said yes! It only took two entire months, lots of diner food, and countless cups of coffee! It was my hope that one day, I would have you as my future wife—with homemade dinners and unlimited cups of coffee…no diner needed.

As we began to date and I got to know you better and better, your inner beauty matched your outer beauty. Not only did I fall for the dimples in your cheeks that ran so deep and the way your long, dark, silky hair fell over your left eye every time you turned your head, you also had an amazing personality that lit up the room. You saw the positives in everything and everyone. It seemed that nothing would get you down. There was a confidence about you when you walked in the room that caused all eyes to stop and turn to look at you. You were talented in so many areas. So intelligent. So strong.

Letter To My Wife

So spiritual. I had to make you my wife and the mother of my future children!

Yvonne Thomas Duhon

"He who finds a wife finds what is good and receives favor from the Lord."
Proverbs 18:22 (NIV)

Letter To My Wife

A year later came the wedding. Our first two years of marriage were great! Our daughter was born later that Summer. Words could not describe the joy I felt in my heart as I held her — that tiny being, one that you and I created. All I could do was stare at her in disbelief. I was so grateful that I was spared from having children with anyone else before I met you. Everything seemed so right and so perfect!

I was so proud to be her father and your husband. I walked around with my head held high and my chest puffed out. At the same time, I was nervous on the inside because I did not know how to be a father. It was a new job for me, and there was no schooling available for the position. No guidebook to follow. No right or wrong way of doing things. I knew that I loved our baby girl, but fatherhood was truly going to be interesting for me. At the time, I had no idea how my past would come back to haunt me and affect my relationship with her.

From our many conversations while dating, you knew that I lost my parents at the age of five from a car crash and that my aunt raised me. You also knew that my aunt and I had a strained relationship because she always seemed so angry and bitter; however, I have always sugar-coated my childhood stories and never wanted to speak in depth about my past.

Yvonne Thomas Duhon

You see, my aunt never had any children from her 13-year marriage to her drunk and abusive husband. I've never admitted to anyone until this very moment that I felt she blamed me for her husband walking out on her. I loved and respected her. I felt that she loved me in her own way, too; yet she was always so cold. Growing up, she took care of me and made sure I was provided for, but we could never seem to bond. Little did I know: Her husband had his own set of issues—including him being sterile—and could never have kids of his own. So, what did he do? He took it out on her by fighting her all the time and getting drunk every weekend.

Every time he looked at me, there was something in his eyes that I just couldn't put my finger on. I later came to find out that he resented me being there. I was the child he could never have. He never even tried to be a father-figure for me. I was to be 'seen and not heard'. His feelings trickled down to my aunt's relationship with me. My presence was a constant reminder to her of the gift she could never give him.

About three years after my aunt took me in, my uncle left her and never came back. She was left to raise me on her own, struggling all along the way. We never had much, but we did always seem to have what we needed. We attended church occasionally. Christmas and birthdays were the only times of the year I would receive gifts. To this day, I still respect my aunt and visit her periodically, helping her out with whatever she needs. Still, we are not any closer than we were when I was a child. It seems she has remained brokenhearted all these years, remaining single, depressed, and bitter.

So, you see, my past played a role in my life as a father. I knew my daughter was a blessing to me, but I didn't know how to be a blessing to her. One thing I adopted from my uncle was that he was a hard worker. Now, that I knew how to be! Despite his evening fights and drunken weekends at home with my aunt, he got up and went to work day after day. Year after year. So, I did what I knew best. I worked…and worked…and worked. It was so much easier to work and let you handle all the rest.

Taking care of home seemed to bring you so much joy, so I allowed you to take the lead in that. Eventually, I found myself taking more and more jobs away from home. I began to love both of you from a distance. I didn't even realize I was doing that. Every time I came home on my weeks off, you would bring it up to me and I would make up excuses as to why I needed to work hard for us. I never paid attention to the fact that I was repeating the very same cycle I grew up in.

Yvonne Thomas Duhon

The distant family relationship.

No father-figure.

The love of materialistic things because I never had much while growing up.

I didn't even realize I was doing anything wrong. I was being what I thought was 'normal'. I knew in my heart that I wanted to be closer as a family than what I had growing up, but I didn't know how to be—neither would my pride ever allow me to openly admit that.

"Children are a gift from the Lord; they are a reward from Him."
Psalm 127:3 (NIV)

As time went by, we noticed that medically, something was not right with our daughter. As she grew, she never seemed to speak. How we longed to hear those precious first words, "Mama" and "Dada". They never seemed to come. We also noticed she seemed to always be startled by loud noises of any kind and was extremely irritable around large crowds. She never seemed to look into our eyes as we gazed into hers.

This is where I remember the beginning of many doctor's visits. Because of my busy career, it was all on you to maneuver your work schedule to accommodate our daughter's many doctor and therapy visits. We were finally told she was diagnosed with 'Autism'. How devastating that news was for me! I had waited years for a child and felt some type of way because of that dreadful diagnosis: Autism. I seemed to do what I did best; I buried that word somewhere down deep and pretended that it wasn't really happening to me. Then, I buried myself in my work.

You were so amazing in how you seemed to make it all look so easy. You went to work. You took care of our daughter. You maintained our home, both inside and out. I never worried about a thing because I knew my wife had it all under control. I would sometimes hear the exhaustion in your voice at night when I would call you while away at work. Nonetheless, I chose to look the other way. How selfish of me! Still, I did nothing to make your days easier.

The weekend of our baby girl's fourth birthday, I thought I was coming home to surprise her. Instead, I was the one who received an unexpected surprise: I was going to be a father again! Twins! I was speechless.

Once again, I had that smile on my face that no one could wipe off. Once again, I walked around with my head held high and my chest puffed out, all the while thinking, *"I am the MAN!"* What an exciting week at home it was for me! It also seemed that therapy was helping our daughter—slowly, but surely. You had invented so many creative ways to communicate with our baby girl, since it appeared the development of her speech was going to take a bit longer than we thought.

I decided to finally take a break from all the traveling for work and spend a few months working from home to prepare us for the twins' arrival that winter, only traveling occasionally when absolutely necessary. I'd never seen you so happy! It was the first time I really paid attention to how tired you looked. The next few months were really good for us! There had been quite a bit of tension between us for a while, with me working away from home all the time.

"For you created my inmost being; you knit me together in my mother's womb. I praise you because I am fearfully and wonderfully made; your works are wonderful, I know that full well."
Psalm 139:13-14 (NIV)

Yvonne Thomas Duhon

It seemed that good times could never hang around for very long. During your second trimester, the doctor noticed there was a problem with not one, but both of our twin sons. They had a heart defect—one worse than the other. Months later, the twins finally made their debut. Our youngest was taken into surgery right away to repair the defect, the oldest having to live with his. The six weeks our youngest son stayed in the Neonatal Intensive Care Unit was hard for all of us, but well worth it! He was a tiny, little thing. So strong. So resilient. So determined. Just like you.

It would be a challenge for you to return to work while trying to juggle all three of our children with their health issues, so you decided to explore your second passion: writing a weekly column for the local paper. That was something you loved and could do from home while still taking care of our kids. It was also time for me to get back on the road to work as well. Once again, I left the majority of duties in your hands. I had spent far too much time at home. I found myself growing irritable because I couldn't go out on a whim like I used to do to buy the latest electronic device that had been released. All of my extra money was spent on diapers, formula, and medical bills. I can't fail to mention I had my eyes set on a new car that was coming out the following year that was definitely going to be in our garage!

You were so busy taking care of everything and everyone else, I paid no attention to the fact that you no longer had time to properly care for yourself. Come to think of it, I couldn't even remember the last time you went to Sunday service or had your regular mid-month brunch with the ladies. I did, however, notice all of your weight gain and that your hair and nails weren't kept up like they used to be. The house seemed to be in disarray all the time. Still, I did nothing, only taking care of half of the "Honey-Do List" you would hand me when I would come home. I still had to have my man-time to relax from work and play with my newest electronic device or catch a game of basketball with the fellas.

I always made time for a family date every time I came home because I really missed all of you so much. I truly loved my family and enjoyed the security I felt from knowing that my home wasn't a broken home. When I would hear that a friend or co-worker was going through a divorce, I felt proud of the fact that I knew my wife and kids were back at home. I was glad their story wasn't our story. I was bringing home a nice-sized paycheck, financially taking care of my family, and doing what I felt my duties were as a man and husband. We went from the smallest house on the block to the largest and always had new cars in the garage. I had all the latest gadgets a guy could ever dream of!

So, what could go wrong with my marriage?

We had our fair share of issues that I considered to be minor. You were a bit of a nag, but weren't all wives? Besides, I worked hard for everything we had, so I deserved to have some perks in our marriage. Was that really too much to ask for? I wasn't even sure why you would get so angry. The complaining and blaming was annoying at times, but surely, I wasn't the problem—or so I thought. What was a few pieces of dirty laundry on the floor after my showers, or not making the effort to go to church with you and the kids when I came home, or missing a few of the kids' milestones or school accomplishments? I didn't see the big deal!

We went on like that for a few more years. Our daughter seemed to finally start blossoming with all the expensive—but much-needed—therapy to help her develop her speech and communication. The special autistic school she attended was also paying off, helping to educate her. Our youngest twin son was thriving, despite the heart condition he was born with.

Unfortunately, our oldest was still struggling with many medical visits, medication, and constant monitoring.

Still, I felt we were doing pretty good in our marriage. From time to time, you would approach me with conversation regarding how to better our marriage, but I felt like, *"If it's not broke, why fix it?"* Clearly, you did not see what I saw. Even my family and friends noticed what a good job I was doing to take care of my family and home.

I guess I must have brushed you off one too many times, because next thing I knew, you were threatening to separate. Being the prideful man that I was, I called your bluff. I was a pretty great catch! What woman wouldn't want me? Handsome. Charming. Hard-working. The head man in charge at my company. I had done pretty well for myself over the years. Clearly, I was every woman's dream!

Yvonne Thomas Duhon

*"The Lord will fight for you;
you need only to be still."*
Exodus 14:14 (NIV)

Nine months later, I couldn't believe you actually went through with it: You walked out on me. I was determined to not live my life like my aunt, ending up bitter, depressed, and alone. If you didn't want me, surely, someone else would! Besides, I had plenty of offers on the table from women I had met through work and my social life outside of work while working away from home. I didn't have to go far to find someone who would appreciate me. It was much simpler to walk away from you than to stick around and work it out. All of that compromising and communication was too much for me! So, walked away I did, never really looking back and wondering how you and the kids were making it, never asking if you needed anything, and never offering either. That really wasn't a worry for me. You had always made it look easy in the past. I knew if anyone could do it, it would be you.

    I would call every few days to talk to the kids and would occasionally pay them a visit, taking them out for a treat for a couple of hours or so—when I had the time in my schedule. I made sure to take care of my financial obligations to them so that they could continue to receive the proper care they were getting for their medical and educational needs. I made up stories along the way about our separation to my family and friends to protect my pride and reputation. Surely, no one would understand why you would leave the fortress of security I had given you on a silver platter!

Life was good for me for a while. Even though I had a lot of bills, I was living the dream life! I continued to move up in my career. I was free of the responsibility of raising my kids and would see them when I had the time. I was traveling and started a new relationship with another woman. It felt good to once again enjoy the newness and fun of a dating relationship. My free time was no longer obligated to completing your "Honey-Do Lists", cleaning up after kids, and listening to a nagging wife. I came and went as I pleased and created a new, safe place for myself. It was so much easier to just send you a check and let you handle the rest. Little did I know: My 'good life' was about to come to a screeching halt!

Almost a year after doing my own thing, I received a phone call from your best friend — a call I will never forget.

"It's cancer", she said tearfully.

I didn't even know you were sick! I had been so preoccupied with living my life, I never paid attention to the signs that were right there all along. That news was heartbreaking for me to hear. Even though I was hurt and angry about our separation, I still loved you. In my mind, I felt you were invincible and would always be okay — with or without me.

That was the first time in a long time that I dropped everything I had going on to make you my priority. It was complicated, especially since I had started a relationship with someone else, but you were still my wife. *"The other woman would just have to understand"*, I told myself. I guess 'complicated' was what I deserved for opening one door before the other was closed.

On my flight home, so many thoughts rushed through my mind. I reflected back on when I first met you and how we arrived at the place where we were now. I also thought about how bad your level of frailty would be and how I would handle seeing that in you. I was not sure I could because I had never been through anything like that before; neither had I ever seen you with anything except the smile that melted my heart, the strength of a thousand women, and your constant positive attitude — no matter how bad things were between us.

Once I landed and jumped in the rental car from the airport, it was then that I broke down. I cried out to God, **"What do I do?"** I felt guilty for being so selfish and arrogant, not truly appreciating the gifts I was blessed with. Spirituality wasn't my strong suit. I believed in God and somewhat knew the Word, but I never prioritized or lived it. While we were dating, I gave you the illusion that I was more spiritual than I actually was. I never prayed with my family and always let you take the lead in that area. All the things I should have been doing from the beginning were about to be dropped into my lap with no warning. I would have to figure it out and try to be half as good as you were at it. It was the scariest feeling in the world because I had become so comfortable in our situation.

"Cast all your anxiety on Him, because He cares for you."
1 Peter 5:7 (NIV)

I was sitting in the driveway, terrified to walk up to the door. At the same time, I wanted to rush in. What do I say? How do I act? Can I keep my composure? Will I break down? So many questions flooded my mind.

It's funny how I seemed to be talking to God so much now. I never did a whole lot of that before, just on occasion. Then, I started to become frustrated. I knew how much you loved the Lord. Where was He now? Surely, you didn't deserve this! Our kids didn't deserve this! What kind of God would give you these kinds of burdens? Ok, God: You have my attention now!

As I walked up to the door, your best friend answered before the first knock. *"Come on in"*, she said. *"She's in the back resting. The chemo and radiation have taken a toll on her strength. The doctor is treating it aggressively since it was caught so late."*

My legs became like cinder blocks as I walked towards the back bedroom. With every step, the anticipation grew and my pulse raced. Then, I saw you. You were sleeping peacefully. I was glad because I didn't want you to see me in a full breakdown. Your beautiful, long, silky dark hair was a distant memory. Only a glimpse of your dimples showed through.

Letter To My Wife

Your skin was darker in appearance, and you were so petite due to the dramatic weight loss.

Just then, you opened your eyes, saw me, and smiled. I fell at your side, feeling ashamed of my behavior and treatment towards you. In that moment, I saw the strong woman I married who no one or nothing could bring down; the woman who saw the negatives in nothing, but the positives in everything. As I knelt at your side, you whispered to me, *"You do not know now what God is doing, but later, you will understand"*. That was the wife I've always known, constantly reciting scriptures and positive quotes. How could I have allowed you to walk away from me? That was all irrelevant now. I'm here. I'm home.

Thank God for your best friend! She did an amazing job holding down the fort on your bad days. Still, she and I would have to sit down later and talk about her not telling me earlier what was going on with your health; although in her mind, I'm sure she felt I didn't deserve to know, considering I was being a selfish and arrogant idiot. She walked me through the routine of what I would need to do on a daily basis to keep up with the housework, bills, taking care of the kids, taking care of you, cooking healthy meals, your doctor appointments as well as the kids'...and the list went on and on. Wow! This was a lot! I thought to myself, *"How did she do all of this?"* It suddenly hit me that I was cheating you in my parenting role by only sending a paycheck.

I moved into the room next to yours and set up my computer to work from home while taking care of you and our kids. I must admit: That was a challenge! I suddenly had great admiration and appreciation for all that you did. Did God really have to show me in this way?

The first couple of nights, I slept in the recliner next to your bed and watched you sleep. I would pick up the Bible that sat on your nightstand and read some of your highlighted passages to you. The scriptures seemed to not only speak to you, but they spoke to me as well. I began to pray nightly to you and over you with our kids. God was using this tragedy to reel me in, since it seemed I wasn't going to do it by myself.

After a week, you began to regain your strength. Your first request was to attend Sunday service. I gladly obliged! It was the first time in years that we attended church together, and God had a message waiting just for me. On that Sunday, the Pastor's sermon was "How Husbands Should Be Loving Their Wives". As I sat and listened, there was a feeling that came over me — one I never really felt before. It was called "Conviction".

Letter To My Wife

Never before had I ever felt bad about disappointing God and my family. It was a lot to take in. I sat there ashamed and angry at myself for what I had done. To sit there, be faced with the truth, and not run away as I usually did really hurt. I wanted to fall on my knees and ask for forgiveness and help to turn my life around; however, the thought of me getting up in front of everyone to accept the invitation to do so was downright frightening. So, I stayed in my seat and did nothing.

On the way home from church, my phone rang—just as it had been doing all week. It was 'her'. How was I going to explain to her that I had moved back home to take care of my wife and kids? I was stuck between two worlds and needed to come up with a game plan before speaking with her, so I avoided answering her calls. I needed more time.

I went about my day making sure you had the comforts you needed because the trip to church was exhausting for you. I took the kids to the park to give you some time to rest because tomorrow was going to start another week of chemo and radiation treatments.

Before I knew it, a month had gone by. Our weekly rituals consisted of me taking care of you, our kids, our home, and church on Sunday (when you were strong enough to make the trip). It had only been a month, and I was exhausted! To think: You had done those things for years!

All throughout that time, I continued to receive calls from 'her'. She had grown impatient and angry. It was time for me to make the dreaded call. I still had feelings for her because she brought something to my life that I no longer experienced with you; but when I sat down and evaluated the pros and cons, what she offered to me was what I wanted but not what I needed in my life. It minored in comparison to what I had with you. I would have to explain that to her. I felt horrible having to hurt her because I started off the relationship with her based on a lie, out of lust, and my selfish gain. As horrible as it hurt — especially me having to deal with what I had done — it was worth getting my family back.

The call went as expected: lots of yelling back and forth, then crying, then having to say it was over. I had to add yet another item to my list to ask forgiveness for from God, but as you have always told me, *"If we confess our sins, He will forgive us and cleanse us from all unrighteousness"*. Finally, that chapter of my life was over. It felt good to have that burden lifted off my shoulders.

"If we confess our sins, He will forgive us and cleanse us from all unrighteousness."
1 John 1:9 (NIV)

We made it through yet another month. I was now more focused with some of my transgressions behind me. I became committed to putting my family back on track. I started to take the lead, as I had not done before, in praying with my family and accepting help from church members. The help came in many forms, but all still useful in helping to build me up to be a better man, father, and husband. Sisters came by a few times a week to drop off hot meals or assist in taking or picking up the kids from school; other times, they came just to sit with you to give me a much-needed break. Brothers came through for me as well, talking with me, counseling me, and lifting me up. What a true family in Christ I had been missing out on all of that time! I was moved by the love being shown. Their attentiveness and sincerity were truly different than what I had while growing up. Had I not constantly run away when tough times came, I could have taken advantage of their kind gestures a long time ago. What mattered most was that I chose to make full use of the golden opportunities presented in that moment.

Truly listening at every church service and applying the Word to my life was refreshing. I finally had the courage and knew beyond a shadow of a doubt that I was ready to turn my life over to God completely. I took the opportunity at the next

Sunday service to do just that. It was another fitting sermon that day. The Pastor spoke on "Salvation and Transformation". As I walked up to the altar, I knew I was doing the right thing. It was a feeling like no other. I became weak in the knees as I approached. Tears ran down my face. I couldn't put into words all that I wanted to say, but I knew God knew and understood what I was feeling in my heart.

The heavy weights I had carried around for years felt so much lighter. To lay my burdens at the altar and know that God would be taking over was comforting. I wanted Him to create a "new me" from that point forward and help me deal with all the dysfunction that had made me the man I was. I was ready to be the man God truly intended me to be. Transformed. A work in progress. I was on my way to an exciting, new journey!

"Blessed is the family that hears the Word of the Lord and obeys it."
Luke 11:28 (NIV)

The next day, we headed to the doctor for an update on your progress with the chemo and radiation treatments. I prayed for God to restore your health and our family. I knew that whatever I asked and believed for in prayer, I would receive.

So, as we sat in the office nervously waiting for the doctor to walk in and give us the news, I was not prepared for what came next: The doctor stated the treatments were not successful! He went on to say that he was going to discontinue all medications and treatments, and that you would be sent back home to rest and be at peace during your last few weeks. I was devastated beyond words. What just happened? It took a moment for it all to sink in. I was overwhelmed with emotion.

Clearly, healing you from cancer was not in God's plan. I knew there was a lesson for me to learn, but I felt that moment was not the time I wanted to learn it. I was just getting my life and family back on track. I must admit: I did not see you being taken from me coming from a mile away. The flesh part of me was so angry at God, and it was fighting with the spiritual side of me that knew God still had a plan and purpose for what was happening.

The words you first whispered to me when I returned home were now haunting me: *"You do not know now what God is doing, but later, you will understand."*

I grew steadily angrier with myself for wasting precious time with the gift He entrusted me with. I had been a terrible steward, even though I was now trying to 'right the wrong'.

The ride home that day seemed longer than ever before. I couldn't speak a word; I just drove in silence. It was now my duty to make these last few weeks the best ever for you and our kids. As the days went by, I did just that. It was amazing how you handled the entire situation. I was truly being taught many lessons.

The 'weeks' I was told by the doctor that we would have with you turned out to be only 'days'. You were at such peace with everything. You simply wanted to rest and no longer be in pain. How could I be selfish and take that from you?

So, 10 days after that last trip home from the doctor's office, I whispered in your ear that the kids and I would be okay and that I am in God's hands now. I finally understood His plan. He would do whatever it took to draw me back to Him. I had gambled with God and lost you in the process.

Letter To My Wife

That night, I called all of the family together. All of us gathered around your bedside and prayed over you. You said to us, *"Please don't cry because I'm dying; smile because I've lived and now that His purpose has been fulfilled, I get to see you again"*. Then, you closed your eyes and slowly slipped away. Even in that moment, you were still that amazing woman I had met years earlier.

As I write this letter to you to place in your coffin, I'm hopeful, grateful, and thankful at the thought that in momentarily losing you, I found me and will now have the opportunity to be with you again.

I will forever love you,

Your Husband

Yvonne Thomas Duhon

*"Blessed are those who mourn,
for they will be comforted."*
Matthew 5:4 (NIV)

About the Author

Yvonne Thomas Duhon is a resident of Lafayette, Louisiana. In addition to being the President and Founder of her non-profit organization known as *The Yvonne Thomas Foundation*, she is also a Christian Fiction Short Story Author with two published books: *Letter To My Husband* and *Letter To My Wife*.

Through her involvement in *The Yvonne Thomas Foundation*, Yvonne inspires, encourages, and mentors young women in the community through private sessions, guest speaking, seminars, and cooking classes. She also regularly volunteers her time to support various community service events, activities, and fundraisers.

Yvonne is also actively-involved in ministry at her church, where she volunteers her time in the Evangelizing Ministry, Culinary Ministry, FUEL Ministry, and church choir. She is passionate about her desire to assist other women to be all God has purposed them to be, and she is on a mission to be the change she wants to see in the world, leading by example.

www.ingramcontent.com/pod-product-compliance
Lightning Source LLC
Chambersburg PA
CBHW071547080526
44588CB00011B/1823